Level 2

The Nature Kid's Guide to
GEESE

DAVID ANDERSON

LP Media Inc. Publishing
Text copyright © 2026 by LP Media Inc.
All rights reserved.

No part of this book may be reproduced or transmitted in any form or by any means, electronic or mechanical, including photocopying, recording, or by an information storage and retrieval system — except by a reviewer who may quote brief passages in a review to be printed in a magazine or newspaper — without permission in writing from the publisher.

For information address LP Media Inc. Publishing,
30012 Variolite St NW, Princeton MN 55371
www.lpmedia.org

Publication Data

Geese
The Nature Kid's Guide to Geese — First edition.

Summary: "Learn all about Geese, the Nature Kid Way"
— Provided by publisher.

ISBN: 979-8-89818-244-1

[1. Geese – Non-Fiction] I. Title.

Title: The Nature Kid's Guide to Geese

CONTENTS

GEESE UNLEASHED

Honk! A Canadian goose flaps hard and lifts into the sky.

Geese are so much more than birds you see at the park. They soar across oceans and over peaks higher than any plane flies. Some live in hot, dry places. Others survive where it snows all winter long.

These tough birds live on every continent but one. You will not find them in Antarctica. But look near any lake, river, or green field, and you might spot a goose.

Geese are strong and smart. They honk loudly to warn each other of danger. They stand up to animals much bigger than them. Get ready to meet some of the world's most amazing birds!

GOOSE GEAR

FUN FACT!

Swoosh! A goose shakes water off its back in a flash.

A goose is built for life on land and water. Its flat, webbed feet work like paddles, pushing the bird through ponds and lakes with ease.

Soft **down** feathers sit close to the skin. They keep the bird warm, even in freezing cold. On top, stiff feathers form a tough, waterproof coat. A single goose has over 25,000 feathers!

A goose also has a wide, flat bill with tiny ridges along the edges. It uses this bill to pull up grass and dig for roots in soft mud. Every part of a goose helps it survive.

FLYING "V"

FUN
FACT!
Geese honk while flying in a V
to cheer each other on—like
teammates at a big game!

Whoosh! A long line of geese cuts across the fall sky.

Geese fly in a shape like the letter V. This is not just for show. The bird in front pushes the air aside, and that helps every bird behind it.

Each goose flies in the **draft** of the one ahead. This saves energy on long trips. The whole flock can fly much farther this way—up to 70 percent farther than a bird flying alone.

The lead bird gets the most tired. So the geese take turns at the front. When one gets worn out, it drops back to rest while another takes over.

NAVIGATION NINJAS

Some geese fly at night when the air is cooler. Cold air is thicker, so their wings work better!

Whoosh! A group of geese drop into a golden rice field in the American South.

Geese **migrate** thousands of miles each year. How do they find their way? They use many tools built right into their bodies.

During the day, geese follow the sun. At night, they use the stars to stay on track. They can even feel the Earth's magnetic pull. It works like a compass inside their head.

Young geese learn the path from their parents. They fly the same routes year after year, and these paths are called **flyways**. Some geese remember landmarks like rivers and mountains along the way.

LOYAL LOVE

12

Ga-ronk! Two geese bow their heads and call to each other.

Most geese pick one partner for life. A pair may stay together for twenty years or more, building nests side by side each spring.

The male guards while the female sits on eggs. He hisses and charges if danger comes near. Both parents work hard to raise their young together.

If one goose gets hurt, the other stays close. Some geese wait for a sick mate to get well before moving on. This strong bond helps the whole family survive.

GOSLING GO!

A gosling can recognize its mother's voice before it even hatches from the egg!

14

Hello world! A tiny gosling breaks out of its shell.

A baby goose is called a gosling. It hatches from an egg after about a month. The tiny chick has soft, yellow fuzz called down.

Goslings can walk and swim within a single day! They follow their mom in a neat little line while the parents lead them to water to find food.

Goslings grow fast. In just two months, they get most of their feathers. By fall, they are ready for their first big flight south with the family.

COMEBACK CHAOS

Honk, honk! A Canada goose charges across the grass.

Canada geese have black heads and white chin straps. They are the best known geese in North America. You can find them in parks, ponds, and fields everywhere.

Long ago, people hunted too many Canada geese. By the early 1900s, the birds almost went extinct. But new laws helped them come back in a big way.

Now there are over 5 million Canada geese. They live in cities and towns, too. Their comeback is one of nature's great success stories.

SNOW GEESE

Snow goose flocks can hold over one million birds— so many they look like a blizzard from far away!

Flap, flap! A snow goose takes to the sky on a winter morning.

Snow geese are named for their bright white feathers. They have black tips on their wings. Some snow geese are a darker blue-gray color instead.

These birds nest in the cold Arctic during summer. When winter comes, huge flocks fly south. Thousands travel together in a big, noisy cloud that can stretch for miles.

Snow geese love to eat roots and shoots. Large flocks can strip a field bare in hours. Too many geese in one spot can harm the land, turning green meadows into mud.

HIMALAYAN HEIGHTS

Bar-headed geese have been spotted flying nearly 30,000 feet high—almost as high as a jet plane!

Fwoosh! A bar-headed goose soars above the tallest peaks.

Bar-headed geese fly higher than almost any bird on Earth. They cross the Himalaya mountains twice a year. Dark bars on their white heads give them their name.

Up high, the air is thin and bitterly cold. Most birds could not breathe up there. But bar-headed geese have special lungs and extra-large hearts. They grab more oxygen with each breath.

These geese breed near lakes in Central Asia. In fall, they fly south over the mountains to reach warm wetlands in India. It is one of the most amazing journeys in nature.

NENE'S COMEBACK

The nene got its name from the soft "nay-nay" sound it makes when it calls.

Squawk! A nene picks its way across dark lava rocks.

The nene is the state bird of Hawaii. It lives on rocky lava slopes and grassy hills. Its feet have less webbing than most geese, which helps it walk on rough ground without slipping.

In the 1950s, only about 30 nene were left in the wild. People had brought cats and rats that ate their eggs. The nene was close to being lost forever.

Helpers stepped in to save them. They bred nene in safe places and set them free. Today, over 3,000 nene roam the islands again. The nene shows what people can do when they work to save a species.

EGYPTIAN ENIGMA

Hiss! An Egyptian goose guards its spot by the river.

Egyptian geese come from Africa. They have brown and tan feathers with dark eye patches. They look like geese, but are actually closer to ducks.

These bold birds are very fierce. They chase away other birds and even people who get too close! Their loud calls echo along rivers and lakes.

Egyptian geese nest in odd places. They use tree holes, rocky cliffs, and rooftops. Long ago, people in ancient Egypt drew these birds on stone walls and temple carvings. They thought the birds were sacred.

PAINTED PLUMAGE

26

Screech! A red-breasted goose calls from the frozen tundra.

Red-breasted geese are some of the most colorful geese alive. Red, black, and white patches cover their chest and face. No other goose looks quite like them.

These small geese breed in the Arctic **tundra** of Siberia. They often build nests near falcon nests on purpose. The fierce falcons scare away foxes that would eat goose eggs.

In winter, red-breasted geese fly to the Black Sea. Sadly, their numbers are going down. People are working hard to protect these beautiful birds before it is too late.

EMPEROR EXPLORERS

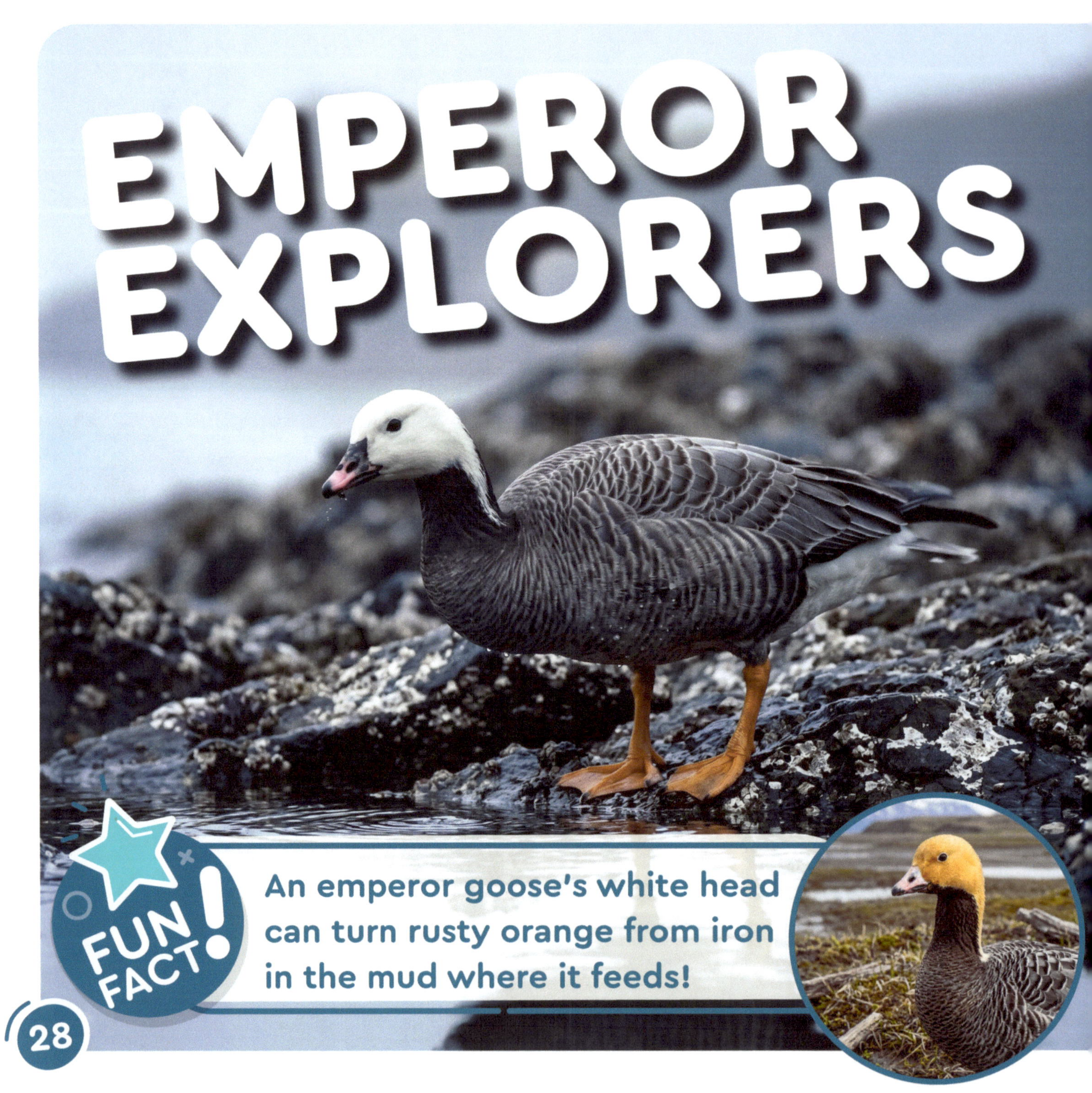

An emperor goose's white head can turn rusty orange from iron in the mud where it feeds!

28

Splash! An emperor goose hunts for clams on the shore.

Emperor geese live along the cold coasts of Alaska. Their gray and white feathers look like tiny fish scales. A bright orange bill and feet make them stand out.

Most geese move with the seasons. But emperor geese stay by the sea all year long. They eat seaweed, clams, and mussels on the beach. Salty water does not bother them at all.

These geese are not often seen by people. They live in far-off places where few roads go, making them one of the least known geese in the world.

GREYLAG GROUPS

The greylag goose gets its name because it always migrates last — lagging behind every other goose species!

Gak-gak! A greylag goose calls out to its big flock.

Greylag geese are big, gray birds with thick orange bills. Most farm geese came from them long ago. Their loud honks can be heard from far away.

These geese live across Europe and parts of Asia. They like open fields near lakes and marshes, where they eat grass, grain, and water plants.

Greylag families stick close together. Grandparents, parents, and young all travel in one group. The older birds help lead the younger ones and teach them where to find food. Family matters to a greylag.

BARNACLE JUMPERS
DID YOU KNOW?
Barnacle goslings weigh less than a tennis ball when they take their death-defying leap!

Look! A barnacle goose tends her chick in a nest high on an Arctic cliff.

Barnacle geese have a white face and black neck. Their body is gray. They nest on steep cliffs in the Arctic, where foxes cannot reach their eggs.

But when the chicks hatch, they must get down. The tiny goslings leap off cliffs up to 400 feet high! They bounce on rocks and tumble through grass. Most survive the big fall because they weigh so little.

Barnacle geese spend winter in Europe. Long ago, people thought they grew from barnacles on driftwood. That silly idea is how they got their funny name.

BRANT'S JOURNEY

Brant geese can fly over 3,000 miles without stopping to rest—that is like flying from New York to London!

Splash! A brant goose drops onto the calm ocean water.

Brant geese are small, dark geese that love the coast. They have a black head, neck, and chest. A small white patch marks the neck. You can often see them bobbing on the waves.

These geese eat mostly eelgrass, a plant that grows in shallow bays. When the tide goes out, brant feed on mud flats. They spend most of their life near salt water.

Brant geese fly long distances each spring and fall. Some travel from Mexico all the way to the Arctic, where they nest on the cold tundra. Then they turn around and do it all again.

GOOSE GUARDIANS

Shoo! A farmer waves her arms to move the geese along.

People and geese have shared the land for ages. In some places, geese help farmers by eating weeds and bugs. In other places, too many geese cause problems for crops and parks.

Wild places where geese live are getting smaller. Wetlands are drying up or being paved over. Dirty water makes some areas unsafe for birds.

Many groups now work to protect geese and their homes. They clean up rivers and guard nesting areas. Everyone can help keep wild geese safe for the future.

BOUNDLESS BIRDS

Some wild geese live over 20 years and may make the same migration journey more than 40 times in their lifetime!

Honk, honk! The geese rise up and head for the horizon.

Geese are truly amazing birds. They fly over the highest mountains and cross oceans. They brave the worst storms. From hot islands to frozen shores, geese find a way to survive.

Every kind of goose has its own story. Some have come back from the edge of extinction. Others still need our help. When we protect wild places, geese can soar.

Next time you hear a honk overhead, look up. A whole flock may be passing by on a trip of thousands of miles. Those birds have made that journey for hundreds of generations.

GLOSSARY

migrate

To travel a long distance with the seasons to find food or a warmer place to live

down

Soft, fluffy feathers close to a bird's skin that trap warmth.

draft

A stream of moving air that birds ride to save energy.

tundra

A cold, flat land in the far north where few trees grow and the ground is often frozen

flyway

A path that birds follow when they travel with the seasons.

www.ingramcontent.com/pod-product-compliance
Lightning Source LLC
Chambersburg PA
CBHW041613110726
48005CB00002B/386